GW00685656

iEdutainments Limited
The Old Post House
Radford Road
Flyford Flavell
Worcestershire
WR7 4DL
England

Company Number: 7441490
First Edition: iEdutainments Ltd 2014

English Version

Illustrated by Andy Garnica

LEARNBOTS®

LEARN 101 ENGLISH VERBS
IN 1 DAY
with the LearnBots

by Rory Ryder

Illustrations Andy Garnica

Published by:

iEdutainments Ltd.

Introduction

Memory

When learning a language, we often have problems remembering the (key) verbs; it does not mean we have totally forgotten them. It just means that we can't recall them at that particular moment. So this book has been carefully designed to help you recall the (key) verbs and their conjugations instantly.

The Research

Research has shown that one of the most effective ways to remember something is by association. Therefore we have hidden the verb (keyword) into each illustration to act as a retrieval cue that will then stimulate your long-term memory. This method has proved 7 times more effective than just passively reading and responding to a list of verbs.

Beautiful Illustrations

The LearnBot illustrations have their own mini story, an approach beyond conventional verb books. To make the most of this book, spend time with each picture and become familiar with everything that is happening. The Pictures involve the characters, Verbito, Verbita, Cyberdog and the BeeBots, with hidden clues that give more meaning to each picture. Some pictures are more challenging than others, adding to the fun but, more importantly, aiding the memory process.

Keywords

We have called the infinitive the (keyword) to refer to its central importance in remembering the 36 ways it can be used. Once you have located the appropriate keyword and made the connection with the illustration, you can then start to learn each colour-tense.

Colour-Coded Verb Tables

The verb tables are designed to save you further valuable time by focusing all your attention on one color tense allowing you to make immediate connections between the subject and verb. Making this association clear and simple from the beginning will give you more confidence to start speaking the language.

LearnBots Animations

Each picture in this book can also be viewed as an animation for FREE. Simply visit our animations link on www.LearnBots.com

Master the Verbs

Once your confident with each colour-tense, congratulate yourself because you will have learnt over 3600 verb forms, an achievement that takes some people years to master!

So is it really possible to "Learn 101 Verbs in 1 Day"?

Well, the answer to this is yes! If you carfully look at each picture and make the connection and see the (keyword) you should be able to remember the 101 verb infinitives in just one day. Of course remembering all the conjugations is going to take you longer but by at least knowing the most important verbs you can then start to learn each tense in your own time.

Reviews

Testimonials from Heads of M.F.L. & Teachers using the books with their classes around the U.K.

"This stimulating verb book, hitherto a contradiction in terms, goes a long way to dispelling the fear of putting essential grammar at the heart of language learning at the early and intermediate stages.

Particularly at the higher level of GCSE speaking and writing, where many students find themselves at a loss for a sufficient range of verbs to express what they were/ have been/ are and will be doing, these books enhances their conviction to express themselves richly, with subtlety and accuracy.

More exciting still is the rapid progress with which new (Year 8) learners both assimilate the core vocabulary and seek to speak and write about someone other than 'I'.

The website is outstanding in its accessibility and simplicity for students to listen to the recurrent patterns of all 101 verbs from someone else's voice other than mine is a significant advantage.

I anticipate a more confident, productive and ambitious generation of linguists will benefit from your highly effective product."

Yours sincerely

Andy Smith, Head of Spanish, Salesian College

After a number of years in which educational trends favoured oral fluency over grammatical accuracy, it is encouraging to see a book which goes back to the basics and makes learning verbs less daunting and even easy. At the end of the day, verb patterns are fundamental in order to gain linguistic precision and sophistication, and thus should not be regarded as a chore but as necessary elements to achieve competence in any given language.

The colour coding in this book makes for quick identification of tenses, and the running stories provided by the pictures are an ideal mnemonic device in that they help students visualize each word. I would heartily recommend this fun verb book for use with pupils in the early stages of language learning and for revision later on in their school careers.

It can be used for teaching but also, perhaps more importantly, as a tool for independent study. The website stresses this fact as students can comfortably check the pronunciation guide from their own homes. This is a praiseworthy attempt to make Spanish verbs more easily accessible to every schoolboy and girl in the country.

Dr Josep-Lluís González Medina Head of Spanish
Eton College

We received the book in January with a request to review it - well, a free book is always worth it. We had our apprehensions as to how glitzy can a grammar book be? I mean don't they all promise to improve pupils' results and engage their interest?

So, imagine my shock when after three lessons with a mixed ability year 10 group, the majority of pupils could write the verb 'tener' in three tenses- past, present and future. It is the way this book colour codes each tense which makes it easy for the pupils to learn. With this success, I transferred the information onto PowerPoint and presented it at the start of each class as the register was taken, after which pupils were asked for the English of each verb. This again showed the majority of pupils had taken in the information.

I sent a letter home to parents explaining what the book entailed and prepared a one-off sample lesson for parents to attend. I had a turnout of 20 parents who were amazed at how easy the book was to use. In March, the book was put to the test of the dreaded OFSTED inspector. Unexpectedly, she came into my year 10 class as they were studying the pictures during the roll call - she looked quite stunned as to how many of the verbs the pupils were able to remember. I proceeded with my lesson and during the feedback session she praised this method and thought it was the way forward in MFL teaching.

Initially we agreed to keep the book for year 10's but year 11 was introduced to the book at Easter as a revision tool. They were tested at the start of each lesson on a particular tense and if unsure were given 20 seconds to concentrate on the coloured verb table and then reciting it. There was a remarkable improvement in each pupils progress.- I only wish we had have had access to the book before Christmas in order to aid them with their coursework- But with this said the school achieved great results. In reviewing the book I would say "No more boring grammar lessons!!! This book is a great tool to learning verbs through excellent illustrations. A must-have for all language learners."

Footnote:

We have now received the new format French and the students are finding it even easier to learn the verbs and we now have more free time.

Lynda McTier, Head of Spanish Lipson Community College

www.learnverbs.com

	Present Simple	Past Continous	Past Simple	Future	Conditional	Present Perfect
I	arrest	was arresting	arrested	will arrest	would arrest	have arrested
You	arrest	were arresting	arrested	will arrest	would arrest	have arrested
He/she/it	arrests	was arresting	arrested	will arrest	would arrest	has arrested
We	arrest	were arresting	arrested	will arrest	would arrest	have arrested
You	arrest	were arresting	arrested	will arrest	would arrest	have arrested
They	arrest	were arresting	arrested	will arrest	would arrest	have arrested

w.learnverbs.com

	Present Simple	Past Continous	Past Simple	Future	Conditional	Present Perfect
I	arrive	was arriving	arrived	will arrive	would arrive	have arrived
You	arrive	were arriving	arrived	will arrive	would arrive	have arrived
He/ she/it	arrives	was arriving	arrived	will arrive	would arrive	has arrived
We	arrive	were arriving	arrived	will arrive	would arrive	have arrived
You	arrive	were arriving	arrived	will arrive	would arrive	have arrived
They	arrive	were arriving	arrived	will arrive	would arrive	have arrived

www.learnverbs.com

	Present Simple	Past Continous	Past Simple	Future	Conditional	Present Perfect
I	ask	was asking	asked	will ask	would ask	have asked
You	ask	were asking	asked	will ask	would ask	have asked
He/ she/it	asks	was asking	asked	will ask	would ask	has aske
We	ask	were asking	asked	will ask	would ask	have asked
You	ask	were asking	asked	will ask	would ask	have asked
They	ask	were asking	asked	will ask	would ask	have asked

www.learnverbs.com

	Present Simple	Past Continous	Past Simple	Future	Conditional	Present Perfect
I	am	was being	was	will be	would be	have been
You	are	were being	were	will be	would be	have been
He/she/it	is	was being	was	will be	would be	has been
We	are	were being	were	will be	would be	have been
You	are	were being	were	will be	would be	have been
They	are	were being	were	will be	would be	have been

www.learnverbs.com

	Present Simple	Past Continous	Past Simple	Future	Conditional	Present Perfect
I	am	was being	was	will be	would be	have been
You	are	were being	were	will be	would be	have been
He/ she/it	is	was being	was	will be	would be	has bee
We	are	were being	were	will be	would be	have been
You	are	were being	were	will be	would be	have been
They	are	were being	were	will be	would be	have been

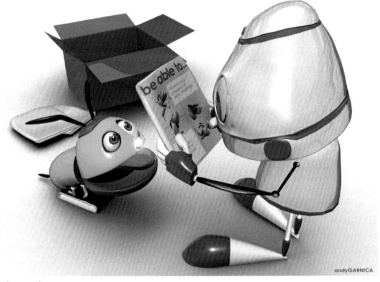

andyGARNICA

www.learnverbs.com

	Present Simple	Past Continous	Past Simple	Future	Conditional	Present Perfect
I	am able (can)	was able	could	will be able	would be able	have been able
You	are able (can)	were able	could	will be able	would be able	have been able
He/ She/it	is able (can)	was able	could	will be able	would be able	has been able
We	are able (can)	were able	could	will be able	would be able	have been able
You	are able (can)	were able	could	will be able	would be able	have been able
They	are able (can)	were able	could	will be able	would be able	have been able

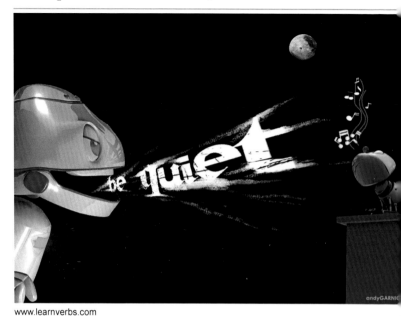

www.learnverbs.com

	Present Simple	Past Continous	Past Simple	Future	Conditional	Present Perfect
I	am quiet	was being quiet	was quiet	will be quiet	would be quiet	have been quiet
You	are quiet	were being quiet	were quiet	will be quiet	would be quiet	have been quiet
He/ she/it	is quiet	was being quiet	was quiet	will be quiet	would be quiet	has been quiet
We	are quiet	were being quiet	were quiet	will be quiet	would be quiet	have been quiet
You	are quiet	were being quiet	were quiet	will be quiet	would be quiet	have been quiet
They	are quiet	were being quiet	were quiet	will be quiet	would be quiet	have been quiet

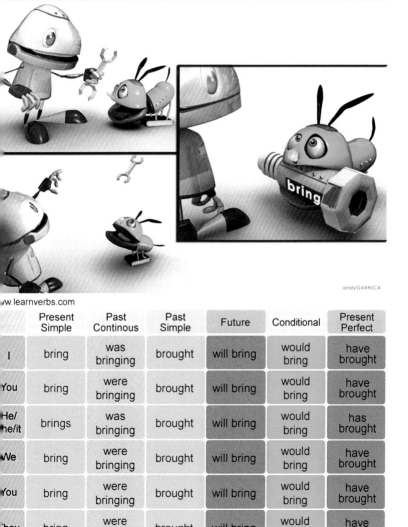

andyGARNICA

www.learnverbs.com

	Present Simple	Past Continous	Past Simple	Future	Conditional	Present Perfect
I	bring	was bringing	brought	will bring	would bring	have brought
You	bring	were bringing	brought	will bring	would bring	have brought
He/ She/it	brings	was bringing	brought	will bring	would bring	has brought
We	bring	were bringing	brought	will bring	would bring	have brought
You	bring	were bringing	brought	will bring	would bring	have brought
They	bring	were bringing	brought	will bring	would bring	have brought

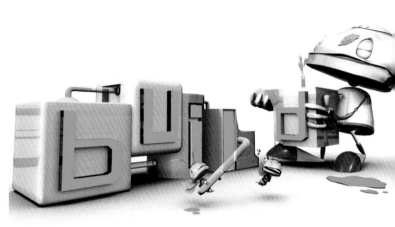

andyGARNIC.

www.learnverbs.com

	Present Simple	Past Continous	Past Simple	Future	Conditional	Present Perfect
I	build	was building	built	will build	would build	have bui
You	build	were building	built	will build	would build	have bui
He/ she/it	builds	was building	built	will build	would build	has bui
We	build	were building	built	will build	would build	have bui
You	build	were building	built	will build	would build	have bui
They	build	were building	built	will build	would build	have bui

www.learnverbs.com

	Present Simple	Past Continous	Past Simple	Future	Conditional	Present Perfect
I	buy	was buying	bought	will buy	would buy	have bought
You	buy	were buying	bought	will buy	would buy	have bought
He/ She/it	buys	was buying	bought	will buy	would buy	has bought
We	buy	were buying	bought	will buy	would buy	have bought
You	buy	were buying	bought	will buy	would buy	have bought
They	buy	were buying	bought	will buy	would buy	have bought

andyGARNICA

www.learnverbs.com

	Present Simple	Past Continous	Past Simple	Future	Conditional	Present Perfect
I	call	was calling	called	will call	would call	have called
You	call	were calling	called	will call	would call	have called
He/ she/it	calls	was calling	called	will call	would call	has calle
We	call	were calling	called	will call	would call	have called
You	call	were calling	called	will call	would call	have called
They	call	were calling	called	will call	would call	have called

www.learnverbs.com

	Present Simple	Past Continous	Past Simple	Future	Conditional	Present Perfect
I	carry	was carrying	carried	will carry	would carry	have carried
You	carry	were carrying	carried	will carry	would carry	have carried
He/ she/it	carries	was carrying	carried	will carry	would carry	has carried
We	carry	were carrying	carried	will carry	would carry	have carried
You	carry	were carrying	carried	will carry	would carry	have carried
They	carry	were carrying	carried	will carry	would carry	have carried

www.learnverbs.com

	Present Simple	Past Continous	Past Simple	Future	Conditional	Present Perfect
I	change	was changing	changed	will change	would change	have changed
You	change	were changing	changed	will change	would change	have changed
He/ she/it	changes	was changing	changed	will change	would change	has changed
We	change	were changing	changed	will change	would change	have changed
You	change	were changing	changed	will change	would change	have changed
They	change	were changing	changed	will change	would change	have changed

www.learnverbs.com

	Present Simple	Past Continous	Past Simple	Future	Conditional	Present Perfect
I	clean	was cleaning	cleaned	will clean	would clean	have cleaned
You	clean	were cleaning	cleaned	will clean	would clean	have cleaned
He/ She/it	cleans	was cleaning	cleaned	will clean	would clean	has cleaned
We	clean	were cleaning	cleaned	will clean	would clean	have cleaned
You	clean	were cleaning	cleaned	will clean	would clean	have cleaned
They	clean	were cleaning	cleaned	will clean	would clean	have cleaned

www.learnverbs.com

	Present Simple	Past Continous	Past Simple	Future	Conditional	Present Perfect
I	close	was closing	closed	will close	would close	have closed
You	close	were closing	closed	will close	would close	have closed
He/ she/it	closes	was closing	closed	will close	would close	has closed
We	close	were closing	closed	will close	would close	have closed
You	close	were closing	closed	will close	would close	have closed
They	close	were closing	closed	will close	would close	have closed

	Present Simple	Past Continous	Past Simple	Future	Conditional	Present Perfect
I	comb	was combing	combed	will comb	would comb	have combed
You	comb	were combing	combed	will comb	would comb	have combed
He/ she/it	combs	was combing	combed	will comb	would comb	has combed
We	comb	were combing	combed	will comb	would comb	have combed
You	comb	were combing	combed	will comb	would comb	have combed
They	comb	were combing	combed	will comb	would comb	have combed

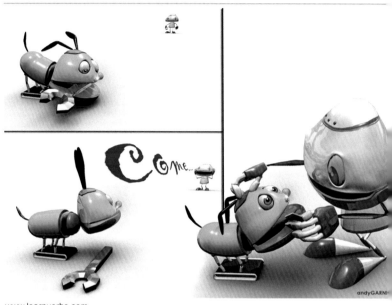

www.learnverbs.com

	Present Simple	Past Continous	Past Simple	Future	Conditional	Present Perfect
I	come	was coming	came	will come	would come	have come
You	come	were coming	came	will come	would come	have come
He/ she/it	comes	was coming	came	will come	would come	has com
We	come	were coming	came	will come	would come	have come
You	come	were coming	came	will come	would come	have come
They	come	were coming	came	will come	would come	have come

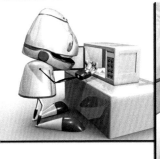

andyGARNICA

www.learnverbs.com

	Present Simple	Past Continous	Past Simple	Future	Conditional	Present Perfect
I	cook	was cooking	cooked	will cook	would cook	have cooked
You	cook	were cooking	cooked	will cook	would cook	have cooked
He/ she/it	cooks	was cooking	cooked	will cook	would cook	has cooked
We	cook	were cooking	cooked	will cook	would cook	have cooked
You	cook	were cooking	cooked	will cook	would cook	have cooked
They	cook	were cooking	cooked	will cook	would cook	have cooked

www.learnverbs.com

	Present Simple	Past Continous	Past Simple	Future	Conditional	Present Perfect
I	count	was counting	counted	will count	would count	have counted
You	count	were counting	counted	will count	would count	have counted
He/ she/it	counts	was counting	counted	will count	would count	has counted
We	count	were counting	counted	will count	would count	have counted
You	count	were counting	counted	will count	would count	have counted
They	count	were counting	counted	will count	would count	have counted

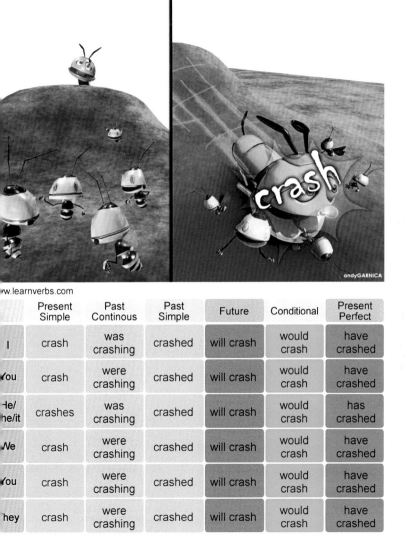

	Present Simple	Past Continous	Past Simple	Future	Conditional	Present Perfect
I	crash	was crashing	crashed	will crash	would crash	have crashed
You	crash	were crashing	crashed	will crash	would crash	have crashed
He/ She/it	crashes	was crashing	crashed	will crash	would crash	has crashed
We	crash	were crashing	crashed	will crash	would crash	have crashed
You	crash	were crashing	crashed	will crash	would crash	have crashed
They	crash	were crashing	crashed	will crash	would crash	have crashed

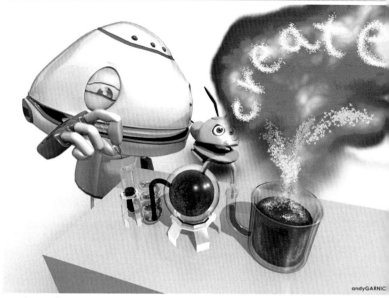

www.learnverbs.com

andyGARNIC

	Present Simple	Past Continous	Past Simple	Future	Conditional	Present Perfect
I	create	was creating	created	will create	would create	have created
You	create	were creating	created	will create	would create	have created
He/ she/it	creates	was creating	created	will create	would create	has created
We	create	were creating	created	will create	would create	have created
You	create	were creating	created	will create	would create	have created
They	create	were creating	created	will create	would create	have created

www.learnverbs.com

	Present Simple	Past Continous	Past Simple	Future	Conditional	Present Perfect
I	cut	was cutting	cut	will cut	would cut	have cut
You	cut	were cutting	cut	will cut	would cut	have cut
He/ She/it	cuts	was cutting	cut	will cut	would cut	has cut
We	cut	were cutting	cut	will cut	would cut	have cut
You	cut	were cutting	cut	will cut	would cut	have cut
They	cut	were cutting	cut	will cut	would cut	have cut

www.learnverbs.com

	Present Simple	Past Continous	Past Simple	Future	Conditional	Present Perfect
I	dance	was dancing	danced	will dance	would dance	have danced
You	dance	were dancing	danced	will dance	would dance	have danced
He/ she/it	dances	was dancing	danced	will dance	would dance	has danced
We	dance	were dancing	danced	will dance	would dance	have danced
You	dance	were dancing	danced	will dance	would dance	have danced
They	dance	were dancing	danced	will dance	would dance	have danced

decide...

andyGARNICA

	Present Simple	Past Continous	Past Simple	Future	Conditional	Present Perfect
I	decide	was deciding	decided	will decide	would decide	have decided
You	decide	were deciding	decided	will decide	would decide	have decided
He/ she/it	decides	was deciding	decided	will decide	would decide	has decided
We	decide	were deciding	decided	will decide	would decide	have decided
You	decide	were deciding	decided	will decide	would decide	have decided
They	decide	were deciding	decided	will decide	would decide	have decided

www.learnverbs.com

	Present Simple	Past Continous	Past Simple	Future	Conditional	Present Perfect
I	direct	was directing	directed	will direct	would direct	have directed
You	direct	were directing	directed	will direct	would direct	have directed
He/ she/it	directs	was directing	directed	will direct	would direct	has directed
We	direct	were directing	directed	will direct	would direct	have directed
You	direct	were directing	directed	will direct	would direct	have directed
They	direct	were directing	directed	will direct	would direct	have directed

ondyGARNICA

www.learnverbs.com

	Present Simple	Past Continous	Past Simple	Future	Conditional	Present Perfect
I	dream	was dreaming	dreamed	will dream	would dream	have dreamed
You	dream	were dreaming	dreamed	will dream	would dream	have dreamed
He/ she/it	dreams	was dreaming	dreamed	will dream	would dream	has dreamed
We	dream	were dreaming	dreamed	will dream	would dream	have dreamed
You	dream	were dreaming	dreamed	will dream	would dream	have dreamed
they	dream	were dreaming	dreamed	will dream	would dream	have dreamed

www.learnverbs.com

	Present Simple	Past Continous	Past Simple	Future	Conditional	Present Perfect
I	drink	was drinking	drank	will drink	would drink	have drunk
You	drink	were drinking	drank	will drink	would drink	have drunk
He/ she/it	drinks	was drinking	drank	will drink	would drink	has drur
We	drink	were drinking	drank	will drink	would drink	have drunk
You	drink	were drinking	drank	will drink	would drink	have drunk
They	drink	were drinking	drank	will drink	would drink	have drunk

	Present Simple	Past Continous	Past Simple	Future	Conditional	Present Perfect
I	drive	was driving	drove	will drive	would drive	have driven
You	drive	were driving	drove	will drive	would drive	have driven
He/ he/it	drives	was driving	drove	will drive	would drive	has driven
We	drive	were driving	drove	will drive	would drive	have driven
You	drive	were driving	drove	will drive	would drive	have driven
hey	drive	were driving	drove	will drive	would drive	have driven

www.learnverbs.com

	Present Simple	Past Continous	Past Simple	Future	Conditional	Present Perfect
I	eat	was eating	ate	will eat	would eat	have eaten
You	eat	were eating	ate	will eat	would eat	have eaten
He/she/it	eats	was eating	ate	will eat	would eat	has eate
We	eat	were eating	ate	will eat	would eat	have eaten
You	eat	were eating	ate	will eat	would eat	have eaten
They	eat	were eating	ate	will eat	would eat	have eaten

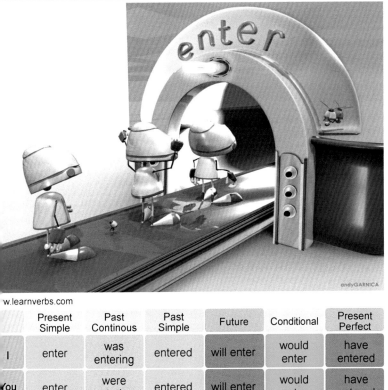

w.learnverbs.com

	Present Simple	Past Continous	Past Simple	Future	Conditional	Present Perfect
I	enter	was entering	entered	will enter	would enter	have entered
You	enter	were entering	entered	will enter	would enter	have entered
He/ She/it	enters	was entering	entered	will enter	would enter	has entered
We	enter	were entering	entered	will enter	would enter	have entered
You	enter	were entering	entered	will enter	would enter	have entered
They	enter	were entering	entered	will enter	would enter	have entered

www.learnverbs.com

	Present Simple	Past Continous	Past Simple	Future	Conditional	Present Perfect
I	fall	was falling	fell	will fall	would fall	have fallen
You	fall	were falling	fell	will fall	would fall	have fallen
He/ she/it	falls	was falling	fell	will fall	would fall	has falle
We	fall	were falling	fell	will fall	would fall	have fallen
You	fall	were falling	fell	will fall	would fall	have fallen
They	fall	were falling	fell	will fall	would fall	have fallen

andyGARNICA

www.learnverbs.com

	Present Simple	Past Continous	Past Simple	Future	Conditional	Present Perfect
I	fight	was fighting	fought	will fight	would fight	have fought
You	fight	were fighting	fought	will fight	would fight	have fought
He/ She/it	fights	was fighting	fought	will fight	would fight	has fought
We	fight	were fighting	fought	will fight	would fight	have fought
You	fight	were fighting	fought	will fight	would fight	have fought
They	fight	were fighting	fought	will fight	would fight	have fought

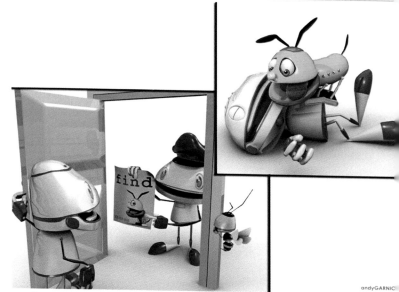

www.learnverbs.com

	Present Simple	Past Continous	Past Simple	Future	Conditional	Present Perfect
I	find	was finding	found	will find	would find	have found
You	find	were finding	found	will find	would find	have found
He/ she/it	finds	was finding	found	will find	would find	has four
We	find	were finding	found	will find	would find	have found
You	find	were finding	found	will find	would find	have found
They	find	were finding	found	will find	would find	have found

	Present Simple	Past Continous	Past Simple	Future	Conditional	Present Perfect
I	finish	was finishing	finished	will finish	would finish	have finished
You	finish	were finishing	finished	will finish	would finish	have finished
He/ she/it	finishes	was finishing	finished	will finish	would finish	has finished
We	finish	were finishing	finished	will finish	would finish	have finished
You	finish	were finishing	finished	will finish	would finish	have finished
hey	finish	were finishing	finished	will finish	would finish	have finished

andyGARNIC

www.learnverbs.com

	Present Simple	Past Continous	Past Simple	Future	Conditional	Present Perfect
I	follow	was following	followed	will follow	would follow	have followed
You	follow	were following	followed	will follow	would follow	have followed
He/she/it	follows	was following	followed	will follow	would follow	has followed
We	follow	were following	followed	will follow	would follow	have followed
You	follow	were following	followed	will follow	would follow	have followed
They	follow	were following	followed	will follow	would follow	have followed

	Present Simple	Past Continous	Past Simple	Future	Conditional	Present Perfect
I	forbid	was forbidding	forbade	will forbid	would forbid	have forbidden
You	forbid	were forbidding	forbade	will forbid	would forbid	have forbidden
He/ She/it	forbids	was forbidding	forbade	will forbid	would forbid	has forbidden
We	forbid	were forbidding	forbade	will forbid	would forbid	have forbidden
You	forbid	were forbidding	forbade	will forbid	would forbid	have forbidden
They	forbid	were forbidding	forbade	will forbid	would forbid	have forbidden

www.learnverbs.com

	Present Simple	Past Continous	Past Simple	Future	Conditional	Present Perfect
I	forget	was forgetting	forgot	will forget	would forget	have forgotte
You	forget	were forgetting	forgot	will forget	would forget	have forgotte
He/ she/it	forgets	was forgetting	forgot	will forget	would forget	has forgotte
We	forget	were forgetting	forgot	will forget	would forget	have forgotte
You	forget	were forgetting	forgot	will forget	would forget	have forgotte
They	forget	were forgetting	forgot	will forget	would forget	have forgotte

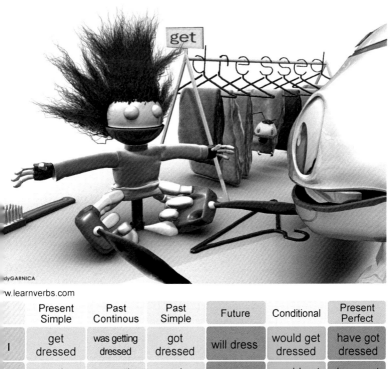

AndyGARNICA

www.learnverbs.com

	Present Simple	Past Continous	Past Simple	Future	Conditional	Present Perfect
I	get dressed	was getting dressed	got dressed	will dress	would get dressed	have got dressed
You	get dressed	were getting dressed	got dressed	will dress	would get dressed	have got dressed
He/ she/it	gets dressed	was getting dressed	got dressed	will dress	would get dressed	has got dressed
We	get dressed	were getting dressed	got dressed	will dress	would get dressed	have got dressed
You	get dressed	were getting dressed	got dressed	will dress	would get dressed	have got dressed
They	get dressed	were getting dressed	got dressed	will dress	would get dressed	have got dressed

www.learnverbs.com

	Present Simple	Past Continous	Past Simple	Future	Conditional	Present Perfect
I	get married	was getting married	got married	will get married	would get married	have go married
You	get married	were getting married	got married	will get married	would get married	have go married
He/she/it	get married	was getting married	got married	will get married	would get married	has go married
We	get married	were getting married	got married	will get married	would get married	have go married
You	get married	were getting married	got married	will get married	would get married	have go married
They	get married	were getting married	got married	will get married	would get married	have go married

	Present Simple	Past Continous	Past Simple	Future	Conditional	Present Perfect
I	give	was giving	gave	will give	would give	have given
You	give	were giving	gave	will give	would give	have given
He/ he/it	gives	was giving	gave	will give	would give	has given
We	give	were giving	gave	will give	would give	have given
You	give	were giving	gave	will give	would give	have given
They	give	were giving	gave	will give	would give	have given

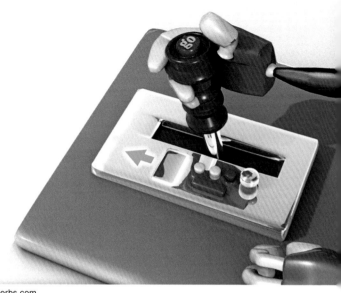

andyGARNICA

www.learnverbs.com

	Present Simple	Past Continous	Past Simple	Future	Conditional	Present Perfect
I	go	was going	went	will go	would go	have gone
You	go	were going	went	will go	would go	have gone
He/she/it	goes	was going	went	will go	would go	has gon
We	go	were going	went	will go	would go	have gone
You	go	were going	went	will go	would go	have gone
They	go	were going	went	will go	would go	have gone

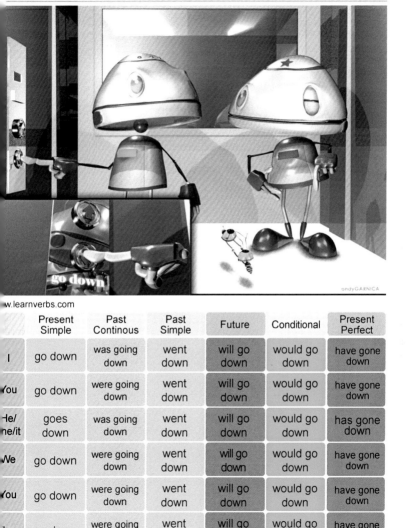

www.learnverbs.com

	Present Simple	Past Continous	Past Simple	Future	Conditional	Present Perfect
I	go down	was going down	went down	will go down	would go down	have gone down
You	go down	were going down	went down	will go down	would go down	have gone down
He/ she/it	goes down	was going down	went down	will go down	would go down	has gone down
We	go down	were going down	went down	will go down	would go down	have gone down
You	go down	were going down	went down	will go down	would go down	have gone down
They	go down	were going down	went down	will go down	would go down	have gone down

www.learnverbs.com

	Present Simple	Past Continous	Past Simple	Future	Conditional	Present Perfect
I	go out	was go out	went out	will go out	would go out	have gone ou
You	go out	were go out	went out	will go out	would go out	have gone ou
He/ she/it	goes out	was go out	went out	will go out	would go out	has gon out
We	go out	were go out	went out	will go out	would go out	have gone ou
You	go out	were go out	went out	will go out	would go out	have gone ou
They	go out	were go out	went out	will go out	would go out	have gone ou

andyGARNICA

www.learnverbs.com

	Present Simple	Past Continuous	Past Simple	Future	Conditional	Present Perfect
I	grow	was growing	grew	will grow	would grow	have grown
You	grow	were growing	grew	will grow	would grow	have grown
He/ she/it	grows	was growing	grew	will grow	would grow	has grown
We	grow	were growing	grew	will grow	would grow	have grown
You	grow	were growing	grew	will grow	would grow	have grown
They	grow	were growing	grew	will grow	would grow	have grown

www.learnverbs.com

	Present Simple	Past Continous	Past Simple	Future	Conditional	Present Perfect
I	have	was having	had	will have	would have	have ha
You	have	were having	had	will have	would have	have ha
He/she/it	has	was having	had	will have	would have	has had
We	have	were having	had	will have	would have	have ha
You	have	were having	had	will have	would have	have ha
They	have	were having	had	will have	would have	have ha

www.learnverbs.com

	Present Simple	Past Continous	Past Simple	Future	Conditional	Present Perfect
I	hear	was hearing	heard	will hear	would hear	have heard
You	hear	were hearing	heard	will hear	would hear	have heard
He/ She/it	hears	was hearing	heard	will hear	would hear	has heard
We	hear	were hearing	heard	will hear	would hear	have heard
You	hear	were hearing	heard	will hear	would hear	have heard
They	hear	were hearing	heard	will hear	would hear	have heard

www.learnverbs.com

	Present Simple	Past Continous	Past Simple	Future	Conditional	Present Perfect
I	jump	was jumping	jumped	will jump	would jump	have jumped
You	jump	were jumping	jumped	will jump	would jump	have jumped
He/ she/it	jumps	was jumping	jumped	will jump	would jump	has jumped
We	jump	were jumping	jumped	will jump	would jump	have jumped
You	jump	were jumping	jumped	will jump	would jump	have jumped
They	jump	were jumping	jumped	will jump	would jump	have jumped

www.learnverbs.com

	Present Simple	Past Continous	Past Simple	Future	Conditional	Present Perfect
I	kick	was kicking	kicked	will kick	would kick	have kicked
You	kick	were kicking	kicked	will kick	would kick	have kicked
He/ she/it	kicks	was kicking	kicked	will kick	would kick	has kicked
We	kick	were kicking	kicked	will kick	would kick	have kicked
You	kick	were kicking	kicked	will kick	would kick	have kicked
They	kick	were kicking	kicked	will kick	would kick	have kicked

www.learnverbs.com

	Present Simple	Past Continous	Past Simple	Future	Conditional	Present Perfect
I	kiss	was kissing	kissed	will kiss	would kiss	have kissed
You	kiss	were kissing	kissed	will kiss	would kiss	have kissed
He/ she/it	kisses	was kissing	kissed	will kiss	would kiss	has kissed
We	kiss	were kissing	kissed	will kiss	would kiss	have kissed
You	kiss	were kissing	kissed	will kiss	would kiss	have kissed
They	kiss	were kissing	kissed	will kiss	would kiss	have kissed

andyGARNICA

www.learnverbs.com

	Present Simple	Past Continous	Past Simple	Future	Conditional	Present Perfect
I	know	was knowing	knew	will know	would know	have known
You	know	were knowing	knew	will know	would know	have known
He/ she/it	knows	was knowing	knew	will know	would know	has known
We	know	were knowing	knew	will know	would know	have known
You	know	were knowing	knew	will know	would know	have known
They	know	were knowing	knew	will know	would know	have known

www.learnverbs.com

	Present Simple	Past Continous	Past Simple	Future	Conditional	Present Perfect
I	learn	was learning	learnt	will learn	would learn	have learned
You	learn	were learning	learnt	will learn	would learn	have learned
He/ she/it	learns	was learning	learnt	will learn	would learn	has learned
We	learn	were learning	learnt	will learn	would learn	have learned
You	learn	were learning	learnt	will learn	would learn	have learned
They	learn	were learning	learnt	will learn	would learn	have learned

www.learnverbs.com

	Present Simple	Past Continous	Past Simple	Future	Conditional	Present Perfect
I	lie	was lying	lied	will lie	would lie	have lied
You	lie	were lying	lied	will lie	would lie	have lied
He/ she/it	lies	was lying	lied	will lie	would lie	has lied
We	lie	were lying	lied	will lie	would lie	have lied
You	lie	were lying	lied	will lie	would lie	have lied
They	lie	were lying	lied	will lie	would lie	have lied

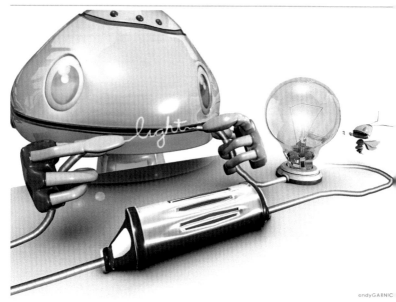

www.learnverbs.com

	Present Simple	Past Continous	Past Simple	Future	Conditional	Present Perfect
I	light	was lighting	lit	will light	would light	have lit
You	light	were lighting	lit	will light	would light	have lit
He/ she/it	lights	was lighting	lit	will light	would light	has lit
We	light	were lighting	lit	will light	would light	have lit
You	light	were lighting	lit	will light	would light	have lit
They	light	were lighting	lit	will light	would light	have lit

www.learnverbs.com

	Present Simple	Past Continous	Past Simple	Future	Conditional	Present Perfect
I	like	was liking	liked	will like	would like	have liked
You	like	were liking	liked	will like	would like	have liked
He/ she/it	likes	was liking	liked	will like	would like	has liked
We	like	were liking	liked	will like	would like	have liked
You	like	were liking	liked	will like	would like	have liked
They	like	were liking	liked	will like	would like	have liked

www.learnverbs.com

	Present Simple	Past Continous	Past Simple	Future	Conditional	Present Perfect
I	lose	was losing	lost	will lose	would lose	have lo
You	lose	were losing	lost	will lose	would lose	have lo
He/ she/it	loses	was losing	lost	will lose	would lose	has los
We	lose	were losing	lost	will lose	would lose	have lo
You	lose	were losing	lost	will lose	would lose	have lo
They	lose	were losing	lost	will lose	would lose	have lo

andyGARNICA

w.learnverbs.com

	Present Simple	Past Continous	Past Simple	Future	Conditional	Present Perfect
I	love	was loving	loved	will love	would love	have loved
You	love	were loving	loved	will love	would love	have loved
He/ She/it	love	was loving	loved	will love	would love	has loved
We	love	were loving	loved	will love	would love	have loved
You	love	were loving	loved	will love	would love	have loved
They	love	were loving	loved	will love	would love	have loved

www.learnverbs.com

	Present Simple	Past Continous	Past Simple	Future	Conditional	Present Perfect
I	make	was making	made	will make	would make	have made
You	make	were making	made	will make	would make	have made
He/ she/it	makes	was making	made	will make	would make	has made
We	make	were making	made	will make	would make	have made
You	make	were making	made	will make	would make	have made
They	make	were making	made	will make	would make	have made

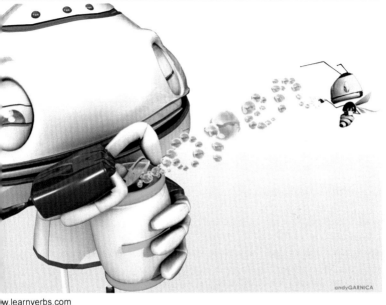

www.learnverbs.com

	Present Simple	Past Continous	Past Simple	Future	Conditional	Present Perfect
I	open	was opening	opened	will open	would open	have opened
You	open	were opening	opened	will open	would open	have opened
He/ she/it	opens	was opening	opened	will open	would open	has opened
We	open	were opening	opened	will open	would open	have opened
You	open	were opening	opened	will open	would open	have opened
They	open	were opening	opened	will open	would open	have opened

www.learnverbs.com

	Present Simple	Past Continous	Past Simple	Future	Conditional	Present Perfect
I	organise	was organising	organised	will organise	would organise	have organise
You	organise	were organising	organised	will organise	would organise	have organise
He/ she/it	organises	was organising	organised	will organise	would organise	has organise
We	organise	were organising	organised	will organise	would organise	have organise
You	organise	were organising	organised	will organise	would organise	have organise
They	organise	were organising	organised	will organise	would organise	have organise

www.learnverbs.com

	Present Simple	Past Continous	Past Simple	Future	Conditional	Present Perfect
I	paint	was painting	painted	will paint	would paint	have painted
You	paint	were painting	painted	will paint	would paint	have painted
He/ She/it	paints	was painting	painted	will paint	would paint	has painted
We	paint	were painting	painted	will paint	would paint	have painted
You	paint	were painting	painted	will paint	would paint	have painted
They	paint	were painting	painted	will paint	would paint	have painted

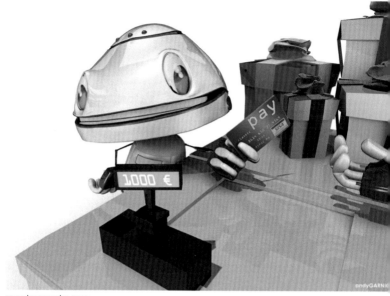

www.learnverbs.com

	Present Simple	Past Continous	Past Simple	Future	Conditional	Present Perfect
I	pay	was paying	paid	will pay	would pay	have pai
You	pay	were paying	paid	will pay	would pay	have pa
He/ she/it	pay	was paying	paid	will pay	would pay	has paid
We	pay	were paying	paid	will pay	would pay	have pai
You	pay	were paying	paid	will pay	would pay	have pai
They	pay	were paying	paid	will pay	would pay	have pai

	Present Simple	Past Continous	Past Simple	Future	Conditional	Present Perfect
I	play	was playing	played	will play	would play	have played
You	play	were playing	played	will play	would play	have played
He/ she/it	plays	was playing	played	will play	would play	has played
We	play	were playing	played	will play	would play	have played
You	play	were playing	played	will play	would play	have played
They	play	were playing	played	will play	would play	have played

www.learnverbs.com

	Present Simple	Past Continous	Past Simple	Future	Conditional	Present Perfect
I	polish	was polishing	polished	will polish	would polish	have polished
You	polish	were polishing	polished	will polish	would polish	have polished
He/ she/it	polishes	was polishing	polished	will polish	would polish	has polished
We	polish	were polishing	polished	will polish	would polish	have polished
You	polish	were polishing	polished	will polish	would polish	have polished
They	polish	were polishing	polished	will polish	would polish	have polished

andyGARNICA

	Present Simple	Past Continous	Past Simple	Future	Conditional	Present Perfect
I	put	was putting	put	will put	would put	have put
You	put	were putting	put	will put	would put	have put
He/ she/it	puts	was putting	put	will put	would put	has put
We	put	were putting	put	will put	would put	have put
You	put	were putting	put	will put	would put	have put
They	put	were putting	put	will put	would put	have put

www.learnverbs.com

	Present Simple	Past Continous	Past Simple	Future	Conditional	Present Perfect
I	quit	was quitting	quitted	will quit	would quit	have quitted
You	quit	were quitting	quitted	will quit	would quit	have quitted
He/ she/it	quits	was quitting	quitted	will quit	would quit	has quitted
We	quit	were quitting	quitted	will quit	would quit	have quitted
You	quit	were quitting	quitted	will quit	would quit	have quitted
They	quit	were quitting	quitted	will quit	would quit	have quitted

	Present Simple	Past Continous	Past Simple	Future	Conditional	Present Perfect
I						
You						
He/ she/it	rains	was raining	rained	will rain	would rain	has rained
We						
You						
They						

www.learnverbs.com

	Present Simple	Past Continous	Past Simple	Future	Conditional	Present Perfect
I	read	was reading	read	will read	would read	have rea
You	read	were reading	read	will read	would read	have rea
He/ she/it	reads	was reading	read	will read	would read	has rea
We	read	were reading	read	will read	would read	have rea
You	read	were reading	read	will read	would read	have rea
They	read	were reading	read	will read	would read	have rea

andyGARNICA

w.learnverbs.com

	Present Simple	Past Continous	Past Simple	Future	Conditional	Present Perfect
I	receive	was receiving	received	will receive	would receive	have received
You	receive	were receiving	received	will receive	would receive	have received
He/ she/it	receives	was receiving	received	will receive	would receive	has received
We	receive	were receiving	received	will receive	would receive	have received
You	receive	were receiving	received	will receive	would receive	have received
They	receive	were receiving	received	will receive	would receive	have received

www.learnverbs.com

	Present Simple	Past Continous	Past Simple	Future	Conditional	Present Perfect
I	record	was recording	recorded	will record	would record	have recorde
You	record	were recording	recorded	will record	would record	have recorde
He/she/it	records	was recording	recorded	will record	would record	has recorde
We	record	were recording	recorded	will record	would record	have recorde
You	record	were recording	recorded	will record	would record	have recorde
They	record	were recording	recorded	will record	would record	have recorde

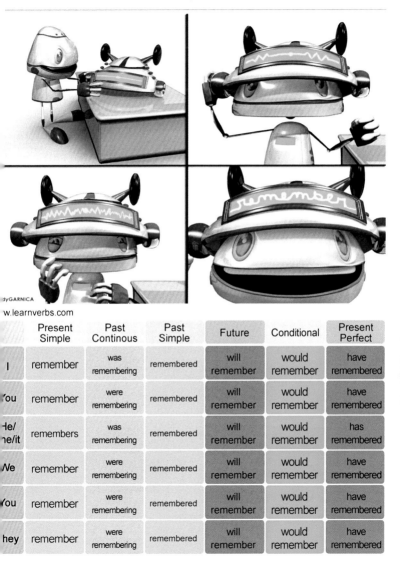

byGARNICA

w.learnverbs.com

	Present Simple	Past Continous	Past Simple	Future	Conditional	Present Perfect
I	remember	was remembering	remembered	will remember	would remember	have remembered
You	remember	were remembering	remembered	will remember	would remember	have remembered
He/ she/it	remembers	was remembering	remembered	will remember	would remember	has remembered
We	remember	were remembering	remembered	will remember	would remember	have remembered
You	remember	were remembering	remembered	will remember	would remember	have remembered
They	remember	were remembering	remembered	will remember	would remember	have remembered

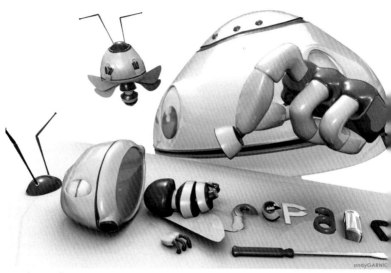

www.learnverbs.com

	Present Simple	Past Continous	Past Simple	Future	Conditional	Presen Perfect
I	repair	was repairing	repaired	will repair	would repair	have repaire
You	repair	were repairing	repaired	will repair	would repair	have repaire
He/ she/it	repairs	was repairing	repaired	will repair	would repair	has repaire
We	repair	were repairing	repaired	will repair	would repair	have repaire
You	repair	were repairing	repaired	will repair	would repair	have repaire
They	repair	were repairing	repaired	will repair	would repair	have repaire

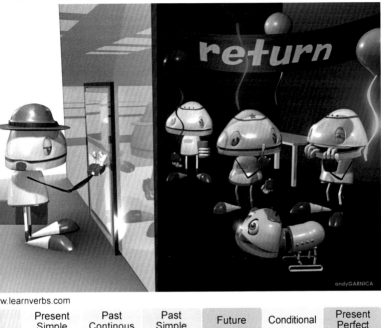

www.learnverbs.com

	Present Simple	Past Continous	Past Simple	Future	Conditional	Present Perfect
I	return	was returning	returned	will return	would return	have returned
You	return	were returning	returned	will return	would return	have returned
He/ she/it	returns	was returning	returned	will return	would return	has returned
We	return	were returning	returned	will return	would return	have returned
You	return	were returning	returned	will return	would return	have returned
They	return	were returning	returned	will return	would return	have returned

www.learnverbs.com

	Present Simple	Past Continous	Past Simple	Future	Conditional	Present Perfect
I	run	was running	ran	will run	would run	have ru
You	run	were running	ran	will run	would run	have ru
He/she/it	runs	was running	ran	will run	would run	has rur
We	run	were running	ran	will run	would run	have ru
You	run	were running	ran	will run	would run	have ru
They	run	were running	ran	will run	would run	have ru

andyGARNICA

w.learnverbs.com

	Present Simple	Past Continous	Past Simple	Future	Conditional	Present Perfect
I	scream	was screaming	screamed	will scream	would scream	have screamed
You	scream	were screaming	screamed	will scream	would scream	have screamed
He/ he/it	screams	was screaming	screamed	will scream	would scream	has screamed
We	scream	were screaming	screamed	will scream	would scream	have screamed
You	scream	were screaming	screamed	will scream	would scream	have screamed
They	scream	were screaming	screamed	will scream	would scream	have screamed

www.learnverbs.com

	Present Simple	Past Continous	Past Simple	Future	Conditional	Presen Perfect
I	search	was searching	searched	will search	would search	have searche
You	search	were searching	searched	will search	would search	have searche
He/ she/it	searches	was searching	searched	will search	would search	has searche
We	search	were searching	searched	will search	would search	have searche
You	search	were searching	searched	will search	would search	have searche
They	search	were searching	searched	will search	would search	have searche

andyGARNICA

w.learnverbs.com

	Present Simple	Past Continous	Past Simple	Future	Conditional	Present Perfect
I	see	was seeing	saw	will see	would see	have seen
You	see	were seeing	saw	will see	would see	have seen
He/ she/it	sees	was seeing	saw	will see	would see	has seen
We	see	were seeing	saw	will see	would see	have seen
You	see	were seeing	saw	will see	would see	have seen
They	see	were seeing	saw	will see	would see	have seen

www.learnverbs.com

	Present Simple	Past Continous	Past Simple	Future	Conditional	Present Perfect
I	separate	was separating	separated	will separate	would separate	have separate
You	separate	were separating	separated	will separate	would separate	have separate
He/ she/it	separates	was separating	separated	will separate	would separate	has separate
We	separate	were separating	separated	will separate	would separate	have separate
You	separate	were separating	separated	will separate	would separate	have separate
They	separate	were separating	separated	will separate	would separate	have separate

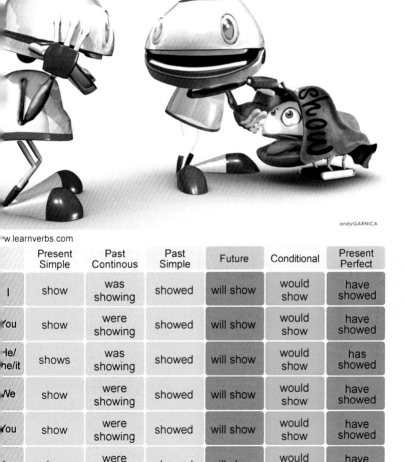

andyGARNICA

www.learnverbs.com

	Present Simple	Past Continous	Past Simple	Future	Conditional	Present Perfect
I	show	was showing	showed	will show	would show	have showed
You	show	were showing	showed	will show	would show	have showed
He/ she/it	shows	was showing	showed	will show	would show	has showed
We	show	were showing	showed	will show	would show	have showed
You	show	were showing	showed	will show	would show	have showed
They	show	were showing	showed	will show	would show	have showed

andyGARNICA

www.learnverbs.com

	Present Simple	Past Continous	Past Simple	Future	Conditional	Present Perfect
I	shower	was showering	showered	will shower	would shower	have showere
You	shower	were showering	showered	will shower	would shower	have showere
He/ she/it	showers	was showering	showered	will shower	would shower	has showere
We	shower	were showering	showered	will shower	would shower	have showere
You	shower	were showering	showered	will shower	would shower	have showere
They	shower	were showering	showered	will shower	would shower	have showere

www.learnverbs.com

	Present Simple	Past Continous	Past Simple	Future	Conditional	Present Perfect
I	sing	was singing	sang	will sing	would sing	have sung
You	sing	were singing	sang	will sing	would sing	have sung
He/ she/it	sings	was singing	sang	will sing	would sing	has sung
We	sing	were singing	sang	will sing	would sing	have sung
You	sing	were singing	sang	will sing	would sing	have sung
They	sing	were singing	sang	will sing	would sing	have sung

www.learnverbs.com

	Present Simple	Past Continous	Past Simple	Future	Conditional	Present Perfect
I	sit	was sitting	sat	will sit	would sit	have sa
You	sit	were sitting	sat	will sit	would sit	have sa
He/ she/it	sits	was sitting	sat	will sit	would sit	has sa
We	sit	were sitting	sat	will sit	would sit	have sa
You	sit	were sitting	sat	will sit	would sit	have sa
They	sit	were sitting	sat	will sit	would sit	have sa

andyGARNICA

w.learnverbs.com

	Present Simple	Past Continous	Past Simple	Future	Conditional	Present Perfect
I	sleep	was sleeping	slept	will sleep	would sleep	have slept
You	sleep	were sleeping	slept	will sleep	would sleep	have slept
He/ he/it	sleeps	was sleeping	slept	will sleep	would sleep	has slept
We	sleep	were sleeping	slept	will sleep	would sleep	have slept
You	sleep	were sleeping	slept	will sleep	would sleep	have slept
hey	sleep	were sleeping	slept	will sleep	would sleep	have slept

www.learnverbs.com

	Present Simple	Past Continous	Past Simple	Future	Conditional	Present Perfect
I	start	was starting	started	will start	would start	have started
You	start	were starting	started	will start	would start	have started
He/ she/it	starts	was starting	started	will start	would start	has started
We	start	were starting	started	will start	would start	have started
You	start	were starting	started	will start	would start	have started
They	start	were starting	started	will start	would start	have started

www.learnverbs.com

	Present Simple	Past Continous	Past Simple	Future	Conditional	Present Perfect
I	stop	was stopping	stopped	will stop	would stop	have stopped
You	stop	were stopping	stopped	will stop	would stop	have stopped
He/ she/it	stops	was stopping	stopped	will stop	would stop	has stopped
We	stop	were stopping	stopped	will stop	would stop	have stopped
You	stop	were stopping	stopped	will stop	would stop	have stopped
They	stop	were stopping	stopped	will stop	would stop	have stopped

www.learnverbs.com

	Present Simple	Past Continous	Past Simple	Future	Conditional	Present Perfect
I	stroll	was strolling	strolled	will stroll	would stroll	have strolled
You	stroll	were strolling	strolled	will stroll	would stroll	have strolled
He/she/it	strolls	was strolling	strolled	will stroll	would stroll	has strolled
We	stroll	were strolling	strolled	will stroll	would stroll	have strolled
You	stroll	were strolling	strolled	will stroll	would stroll	have strolled
They	stroll	were strolling	strolled	will stroll	would stroll	have strolled

www.learnverbs.com

	Present Simple	Past Continous	Past Simple	Future	Conditional	Present Perfect
I	study	was studying	studied	will study	would study	have studied
You	study	were studying	studied	will study	would study	have studied
He/ she/it	studies	was studying	studied	will study	would study	has studied
We	study	were studying	studied	will study	would study	have studied
You	study	were studying	studied	will study	would study	have studied
They	study	were studying	studied	will study	would study	have studied

www.learnverbs.com

	Present Simple	Past Continous	Past Simple	Future	Conditional	Present Perfect
I	swim	was swimming	swam	will swim	would swim	have swum
You	swim	were swimming	swam	will swim	would swim	have swum
He/ she/it	swims	was swimming	swam	will swim	would swim	has swum
We	swim	were swimming	swam	will swim	would swim	have swum
You	swim	were swimming	swam	will swim	would swim	have swum
They	swim	were swimming	swam	will swim	would swim	have swum

w.learnverbs.com

	Present Simple	Past Continous	Past Simple	Future	Conditional	Present Perfect
I	talk	was talking	talked	will talk	would talk	have talked
You	talk	were talking	talked	will talk	would talk	have talked
He/ she/it	talks	was talking	talked	will talk	would talk	has talked
We	talk	were talking	talked	will talk	would talk	have talked
You	talk	were talking	talked	will talk	would talk	have talked
They	talk	were talking	talked	will talk	would talk	have talked

www.learnverbs.com

	Present Simple	Past Continous	Past Simple	Future	Conditional	Present Perfect
I	test	was testing	tested	will test	would test	have tested
You	test	were testing	tested	will test	would test	have tested
He/ she/it	tests	was testing	tested	will test	would test	has tested
We	test	were testing	tested	will test	would test	have tested
You	test	were testing	tested	will test	would test	have tested
They	test	were testing	tested	will test	would test	have tested

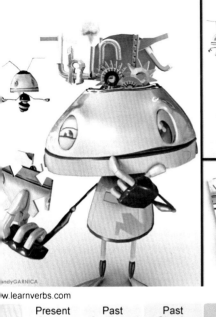

andyGARNICA

w.learnverbs.com

	Present Simple	Past Continous	Past Simple	Future	Conditional	Present Perfect
I	think	was thinking	thought	will think	would think	have thought
You	think	were thinking	thought	will think	would think	have thought
He/ he/it	thinks	was thinking	thought	will think	would think	has thought
We	think	were thinking	thought	will think	would think	have thought
You	think	were thinking	thought	will think	would think	have thought
hey	think	were thinking	thought	will think	would think	have thought

www.learnverbs.com

andyGARNIC

	Present Simple	Past Continous	Past Simple	Future	Conditional	Presen Perfect
I	travel	was travelling	travelled	will travel	would travel	have travelle
You	travel	were travelling	travelled	will travel	would travel	have travelle
He/ she/it	travels	was travelling	travelled	will travel	would travel	has travelle
We	travel	were travelling	travelled	will travel	would travel	have travelle
You	travel	were travelling	travelled	will travel	would travel	have travelle
They	travel	were travelling	travelled	will travel	would travel	have travelle

andyGARNICA

www.learnverbs.com

	Present Simple	Past Continous	Past Simple	Future	Conditional	Present Perfect
I	trip	was tripping	tripped	will trip	would trip	have tripped
You	trip	were tripping	tripped	will trip	would trip	have tripped
He/ she/it	trips	was tripping	tripped	will trip	would trip	has tripped
We	trip	were tripping	tripped	will trip	would trip	have tripped
You	trip	were tripping	tripped	will trip	would trip	have tripped
They	trip	were tripping	tripped	will trip	would trip	have tripped

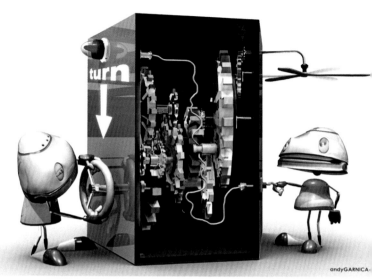

andyGARNICA-

www.learnverbs.com

	Present Simple	Past Continous	Past Simple	Future	Conditional	Present Perfect
I	turn	was turning	turned	will turn	would turn	have turned
You	turn	were turning	turned	will turn	would turn	have turned
He/ she/it	turns	was turning	turned	will turn	would turn	has turned
We	turn	were turning	turned	will turn	would turn	have turned
You	turn	were turning	turned	will turn	would turn	have turned
They	turn	were turning	turned	will turn	would turn	have turned

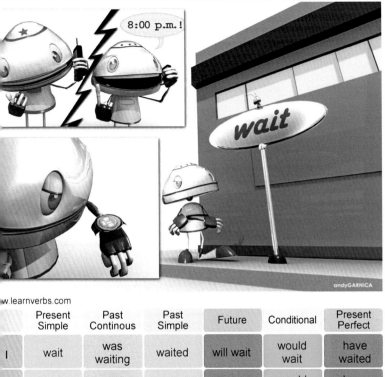

	Present Simple	Past Continous	Past Simple	Future	Conditional	Present Perfect
I	wait	was waiting	waited	will wait	would wait	have waited
You	wait	were waiting	waited	will wait	would wait	have waited
He/ She/it	waits	was waiting	waited	will wait	would wait	has waited
We	wait	were waiting	waited	will wait	would wait	have waited
You	wait	were waiting	waited	will wait	would wait	have waited
They	wait	were waiting	waited	will wait	would wait	have waited

www.learnverbs.com

	Present Simple	Past Continous	Past Simple	Future	Conditional	Present Perfect
I	wake up	was waking up	woke up	will wake up	would wake up	have woken u
You	wake up	were waking up	woke up	will wake up	would wake up	have woken u
He/ she/it	wakes up	was waking up	woke up	will wake up	would wake up	has woken u
We	wake up	were waking up	woke up	will wake up	would wake up	have woken u
You	wake up	were waking up	woke up	will wake up	would wake up	have woken u
They	wake up	were waking up	woke up	will wake up	would wake up	have woken u

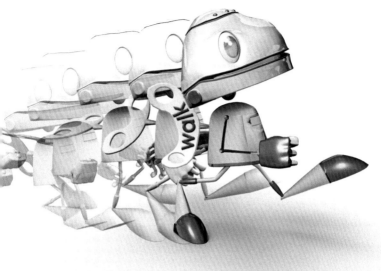

andyGARNICA

	Present Simple	Past Continous	Past Simple	Future	Conditional	Present Perfect
I	walk	was walking	walked	will walk	would walk	have walked
You	walk	were walking	walked	will walk	would walk	have walked
He/ she/it	walks	was walking	walked	will walk	would walk	has walked
We	walk	were walking	walked	will walk	would walk	have walked
You	walk	were walking	walked	will walk	would walk	have walked
They	walk	were walking	walked	will walk	would walk	have walked

www.learnverbs.com

	Present Simple	Past Continous	Past Simple	Future	Conditional	Presen Perfect
I	want	was wanting	wanted	will want	would want	have wanted
You	want	were wanting	wanted	will want	would want	have wanted
He/ she/it	wants	was wanting	wanted	will want	would want	has wanted
We	want	were wanting	wanted	will want	would want	have wanted
You	want	were wanting	wanted	will want	would want	have wanted
They	want	were wanting	wanted	will want	would want	have wanted

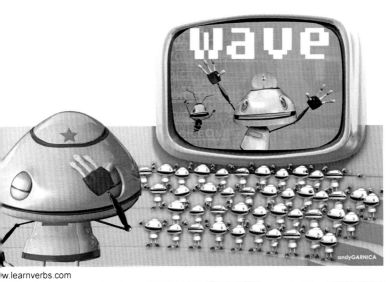

www.learnverbs.com

	Present Simple	Past Continous	Past Simple	Future	Conditional	Present Perfect
I	wave	was waving	waved	will wave	would wave	have waved
You	wave	were waving	waved	will wave	would wave	have waved
He/ she/it	waves	was waving	waved	will wave	would wave	has waved
We	wave	were waving	waved	will wave	would wave	have waved
You	wave	were waving	waved	will wave	would wave	have waved
They	wave	were waving	waved	will wave	would wave	have waved

www.learnverbs.com

	Present Simple	Past Continous	Past Simple	Future	Conditional	Presen Perfect
I	watch	was watching	watched	will watch	would watch	have watche
You	watch	were watching	watched	will watch	would watch	have watche
He/ she/it	watches	was watching	watched	will watch	would watch	has watche
We	watch	were watching	watched	will watch	would watch	have watche
You	watch	were watching	watched	will watch	would watch	have watche
They	watch	were watching	watched	will watch	would watch	have watche

andyGARNICA

w.learnverbs.com

	Present Simple	Past Continous	Past Simple	Future	Conditional	Present Perfect
I	win	was winning	won	will win	would win	have won
You	win	were winning	won	will win	would win	have won
He/ she/it	wins	was winning	won	will win	would win	has won
We	win	were winning	won	will win	would win	have won
You	win	were winning	won	will win	would win	have won
They	win	were winning	won	will win	would win	have won

andyGARNICA

www.learnverbs.com

	Present Simple	Past Continous	Past Simple	Future	Conditional	Present Perfect
I	write	was writing	wrote	will write	would write	have written
You	write	were writing	wrote	will write	would write	have written
He/ she/it	writes	was writing	wrote	will write	would write	has written
We	write	were writing	wrote	will write	would write	have written
You	write	were writing	wrote	will write	would write	have written
They	write	were writing	wrote	will write	would write	have written

Index

English

to arrest	1
to arrive	2
to ask (for)	3
to be	4
to be	5
to be able	6
to be quiet	7
to bring	8
to build	9
to buy	10
to call	11
to carry	12
to change	13
to clean	14
to close	15
to comb	16
to come	17
to cook	18
to count	19
to crash	20
to create	21
to cut	22
to dance	23
to decide	24
to direct	25
to dream	26
to drink	27
to drive	28
to eat	29
to enter	30
to fall	31
to fight	32
to find	33
to finish	34
to follow	35
to forbid	36
to forget	37
to get dressed	38
to get married	39
to give	40
to go	41
to go down	42
to go out	43
to grow	44
to have	45
to hear	46
to jump	47
to kick	48
to kiss	49
to know	50
to learn	51
to lie	52
to light	53
to like	54
to lose	55
to love	56
to make	57
to open	58
to organise	59
to paint	60
to pay	61
to play	62
to polish	63
to put	64
to quit	65
to rain	66
to read	67
to receive	68
to record	69
to remember	70
to repair	71
to return	72
to run	73
to scream	74
to search	75
to see	76
to separate	77
to show	78
to shower	79
to sing	80
to sit	81
to sleep	82
to start	83
to stop	84
to stroll	85
to study	86
to swim	87
to talk	88
to test	89
to think	90
to travel	91
to trip	92
to turn	93
to wait	94
to wake up	95
to walk	96
to want	97
to wave	98
to watch	99
to win	100
to write	101